The Million Stories of Marco Polo

1000000

Michael J. Rosen   illustrated by Maria Cristina Pritelli

Creative Editions

Edited by Kate Riggs   Designed by Rita Marshall

Published in 2016 by Creative Editions

P.O. Box 227, Mankato, MN 56002 USA

Creative Editions is an imprint of The Creative Company

www.thecreativecompany.us

Printed in China

Library of Congress Cataloging-in-Publication Data

Name: Rosen, Michael J.

Title: The Million Stories of Marco Polo / by Michael J. Rosen; illustrated by Maria Cristina Pritelli.

Summary: Among the millions of stories ever told, the tales of the legendary explorer
Marco Polo are the most renowned. Listen as an old-time scribe tells his curious
young neighbor about stories that are worth remembering.

Identifiers: LCCN 2015047478 / ISBN 978-1-56846-290-5

Subjects: LCSH: Polo, Marco, 1254-1323?. Travels of Marco Polo—Juvenile literature.
Polo, Marco, 1254-1323?—Travel—China—Juvenile literature. / Rusticiano da Pisa—Juvenile literature.

Classification: G370.P9 R66 2016 / 910.4—dc23

First edition 9 8 7 6 5 4 3 2 1

Foreword

Marco Polo (1254–1324) was born in Venice, Italy, into a distinguished merchant family. His father and uncle traveled the Middle East and Asia, seeking trade opportunities. At age 17, Marco joined them, embarking on a three-and-a-half-year, 5,600-mile voyage to the court of Emperor Kublai Khan. The elder Polos had met the powerful Khan before and had been asked to return.

Marco soon impressed the Khan with his talents for language and observation. The emperor sent Marco on special missions to the remote and curious cultures that he himself had never seen. In return, Marco regaled Kublai Khan with detailed stories for 17 years. The Polos became important officials of the court as they earned the Khan's trust.

The famed explorers had not planned to be gone for so long. But by 1292, they found their ticket home: they would escort a Mongolian princess to Persia for her wedding. Nearly three years later, they arrived in Venice; Marco was 44. In 1298, Marco engaged in the battles between Venice and Genoa, a neighboring city-state. He was captured. During his yearlong imprisonment, he dictated his travel memoirs to an author, fellow inmate Rustichello da Pisa. Marco lived until 1324, but little is known of his later life.

Although Rustichello's original manuscript of Marco's stories was lost, nearly 150 unique editions of his *Description of the World* exist today. Varied in translation, length, content, and style, each was copied to suit the tastes of the patron or sponsor—the person who paid a scribe to copy down the story. Before the invention of printing presses around 1440, a book was created entirely by hand. Scribes hand-lettered each word, and the pages were then sewn together. As Marco's adventures later spread in printed form, doubts about their authenticity and accuracy grew. Indeed, the book came to be known as *Il milione* (The million lies) in Italian.

The book you are about to read tells a story *about* telling Marco Polo's stories. That's just what Rustichello and other scribes and translators did. Indeed, all of history is a collection of such stories we have come to believe. Perhaps none is grander than the tales of Marco Polo.

"I'm so lucky to live here in Venice! I can walk down my own street to visit a scribe who copied Marco Polo's stories into a book. Like the tale about the elephants that brought the world's tallest trees to Kublai Khan's palace."

"Oh, I am but one scribe, child. And you are but one listener—true, you *are* the one who is most captivated—and the stories of Polo travel far, far beyond our city."

"Does everyone believe them? My father doesn't. He says, 'Trees cannot ride on elephants—*for weeks!*'"

"Yet in the Green Palace where the Emperor spent his summers, Marco witnessed trees of every green shade, forever in leaf. Did they appear by magic … or by elephant?"

7

"Elephant! Still ... some cities Polo visited for the Emperor *do* sound magical. Maybe *you* exaggerate when you tell me the stories. Maybe you added *your* words when you copied the book."

"No, my favorite, my most curious visitor, what I lettered on each page was exactly what Rustichello wrote as he listened to Polo's stories with the other prisoners."

"But how could Polo have remembered 17 years' worth of stories before he returned to Venice?"

"He couldn't."

"Maybe, Polo forgot a million *other* stories?"

"Perhaps. But some sights were surely *burned* into his memories. Some stories he could never forget. In Greater Hermenia, Polo witnessed fountains of black oil spewing from the ground! Unlike the familiar edible oil of olives, this oil *burned*, delivering heat and light. Could *you* forget such a sight?"

"*I would* remember that! What's another story Polo couldn't forget?"

"In the port of Hormos, scorching breezes rage so hot that people run to the countryside to escape them. To keep these so-called Flame Winds from baking their skins, they leap into nearby streams—just their noses poking above water."

"Like an elephant bathing? Was that where Polo saw more elephants?"

"If *you* were Polo, instead of silks and jewels, you'd seek out stories of elephants! But what about those stories you *didn't* seek? Why not ask about Camandi? About its high walls built of earth and fear—about the sorcery that shrouds daytime in darkness so that a thousand bandits can ride, unseen, into the city and no one escapes the plundering? Camandi is not fascinating enough?"

"Daytime darkness? That's a dream! Or a lie! A made-up story, for sure! And there can't be a *million* stories ... even if every day brought a new one and Polo's travels spanned 100 years! How can you know if they're true?"

"I can't *know*, but I can *believe*. Believing makes things true. Now come another time and let me do my copying today. Although this book hardly fascinates like Polo's, I must do my work."

"It's me again! I need you to help me remember another story—exactly!"

"Oh, but my recalling could be wrong! Memory's bucket has a hole, even when it seems full.

"Let's test *your* memory: Where did Polo see disappearing bridges?"

"Badakshan! There, houses perch on mountaintops like falcons upon treetops. And only the king may own the precious lapis lazuli of its mines!"

"What about the bridges?"

"Oh, yes! After the fewest steps onto the bridge, only mist and fog and the promise of nowhere welcomed Polo. The way ahead *vanished*!"

"You are becoming a storyteller, too."

"Maybe bridges vanished because his eyes were so tired from travel?"

"Yes! Tired of treacherous roads! Weary of brutal weather! Polo found no house, no food—no bird that dared fly—at the snow-capped Roof of the World. Centuries of camels had trampled those mountain paths into crumbs, and winds blustered so bitterly, no fires would burn!"

"If I were Polo, I'd have closed my eyes and missed everything!"

"However, in the Province of Darkness, eyes are no help. Sun, moon, star—not one shines. The people live as hunters in ever-twilight, beset by marauders who raid their dwellings of fox and sable furs."

"If it's that dark, how ever do they find their way out?"

"The clever Tartars ride mares whose foals they also bring and secure at the border. Once they've obtained their plunder, the robbers drop the reins and the mares eagerly find their way back to their young and to the light."

"Why are there so many cities of darkness and night?"

"One story just reminds me of another as I recall them for you.
"At the White Feast, it's not dark. It's only white—for luck! A
parade of 100,000 white horses and 5,000 elephants, costumed
in white, all carry furniture and dishes and delicacies for the
Emperor's new year celebration."

"The whole kingdom? From where did all that white cloth come?
And all those horses? Were there black horses and tan horses,
too ... somewhere else? Did Kublai Khan own so many ... of everything?"

"Try imagining the Emperor's hunt. An all-red battalion—10,000 men and 5,000 mastiffs—marches right. An equal battalion, in blue, marches left. Each captures 1,000 beasts each day.

"To the ocean, he brings 500 falcons and 20,000 men to collect the prey.

"And, always, Kublai Khan rides in his chamber of tiger skins and beaten gold atop four elephants."

"Yes, more stories of his elephants!"

27

"Enough elephants, dear child! Even greater are the houses of Cambulac. They surpass the possible: Every gate opens into another city that counts even more people on the other side."

"That's no city—it must be a legend."

"Yet it exists: a never-ending marketplace! A pageant of merchants and travelers, buying, selling, and bartering. Each day, 1,000 cart-loads of silk enter the city."

"Imagine visiting our Venice for the first time ... our streets are paved with seawater, our citizens travel by boats. Those you told of our city—wouldn't they call it a legend? A lie?"

"But, I wouldn't be lying ..."

"Was Polo lying of Suju? Built upon a sea crowded with mountains, a maze of 6,000 bridges—tall enough for ships to pass beneath—unite its sprawling population."

"Pick another of the million stories! I want to hear more!"

"You're like the Emperor! His ears wanted to feast upon Polo's words forever. But forever was too long for Polo."

"So, no more stories?"

"Yes, more stories! *Yours!* Every question begins a voyage. *You* can be Marco Polo now."

Notes

8–9: Most scholars suggest that Polo intended that his "ghostwriter," Rustichello, would embellish his stories in order to give them a more exciting and popular feel.

10–11: While in Greater Hermenia, among the mountains where it is said Noah's ark came to land after the flood, Polo saw geysers of crude oil. It flowed so strongly, he said, that it could fill a ship's hold every day. People traveled from far and wide to gather the fuel. At the time, this oil was also used as a salve to heal wounds on camels.

12–13: Polo traveled twice across Hormos on his travels to and from Cathay, what Polo called northern China, which was at that time controlled by Kublai Khan. Traders arrived at this port in ships filled with silks, gold, spices, and gemstones. But, from June to September, the unbearably hot Flame Wind scorched all life in its path.

14–15: Scholars suggest that the spell of darkness under which the raiders rode into Camandi was likely a very dense smoke from fires created by naphtha, a flammable mixture of natural gas, oil, coal, and peat.

18–19: The mountains of the Badakshan contained gems mined exclusively for the king, including lapis lazuli: a rare blue stone mottled with brassy veins. The king ensured its preciousness by allowing only a few stones—most bestowed as his gifts—to leave his possession.

20–21: The Pamir Mountains of central Asia, nicknamed the "Roof of the World," endure bitterly cold and exceptionally long winters. Some of the world's largest glaciers nest among their peaks. Such high altitudes contain less oxygen—a necessary factor in combustion—and so fire cannot burn well.

22–23: "Tartar" is a historical name for the Mongolian and Turkish peoples of central Asia who were ruled and moved westward by the Khans.

24–25: Chinese New Year coincides with the start of a new calendar year based on the moon's cycles. The 15-day holiday honors ancestors and deities and often includes parades, fireworks, and festive meals. One ancient form of fireworks, sky lanterns or fire balloons, are made of paper walls on a bamboo frame. A candle set inside heats the air and, because warm air rises, causes the lantern to climb higher and higher until it burns to ash in the sky.

28–29: Cambulac was the capital of the Mongolian Empire and main residence of its first ruler, Genghis Khan. Indeed, the city's name translates as "City of the Khan." Cambulac is located at the center of China's present capital, Beijing.